BY THE RIVERS OF BABYLON
Singing the Blues

Printed in the United States of American

Library of Congress Cataloging in Publication Data

By The Rivers of Babylon: Singing The Blues
1. Prose-Poetry.
2. Sacred prose- reflections.
3. African American Poetry.
Taylor, Gregory Lind, Sr., 1951 -

ISBN: 1-4196-0278-0
Library of Congress Txu1-066-518

To order additional copies, please contact us.
BookSurge, LLC
www.booksurge.com
1-866-308-6235
orders@booksurge.com

BY THE RIVERS OF BABYLON
OF BABYLON
Singing the Blues
Why I Sing the Blues

G. L. Taylor

2005

BY THE RIVERS OF BABYLON
Singing the Blues

Contents

Acknowledgements   xi

Why I Sing The Blues: The Search For Meaning
Prose
    I   5
    II   9
    III   13
    IV   17
    V   21

Poetry
The Constitutional Blues   27
del rio L.A. Blues   29
The Yule Tide Blues   31
Just Wondering   33
Getting It Too
    No. 1   35
    No. 2   37
    No. 3   39
    No. 4   41
I Saw Her Today   43
Premonition   45

When The Heart Bleeds Blue: The Search For Love
Prose
    I   51
    II   55
    III   59

Poetry

The Long Search   65
The Blues is   69
Fears   71
Wearing It Well   73
The Wind Sings of Love   75
Deez   77
The Cure For My Blues   79

Acknowledgement

Special thanks to:

Larry Aubry, Gary Batchelor, Jarvis Collier,
Joseph Maizlish, Vicki Phillips, Sharon Weininger and Jagrea
Taylor

To my friend Margie – The Blues Singer, whom when nothing
was funny, and when we were in pain, we laughed and we
cried; yet she reminded me that, 'God is a good God,' and, 'He
knows… just how much we can bear.'

Much love to my three brothers: Jarvis, Louis and Gerald.

To my wife LaRetta, whose love has brought brighter notes into my existence.

Why I Sing The Blues:*The Search for Meaning*

PROSE

Why I Sing The Blues

I

Oh that my head were waters,
and mine eyes a fountain of tears,
that I might weep day and night
for the slain of the daughter
of my people!
-Jeremiah 9:1

5

Faith, for many of us—who have been denied access into the whole of humanity, and lied to regarding our own being—is a darkened pilgrimage through life's backyard.

Our despair and thirst for hope, has set our course, directed our journey; sending us down society's broken alleyways in search of discarded fragments of truths.

And so we have found, that in the hands of the vanquished, these jettisoned scraps have become sacred morsels of salvation.

II

Let that day perish wherein I was born,
and the night in which it was said,
There is a man child conceived.
-Job 3:3

The blues are those rhythmic utterances of an isolated and disenfranchised rabble, who became dislocated and separated from their sacred nursing ground—their primordial community.

They are but the songs of sorrow, which emerges from a soul turned sour; the discarded staccato notes of a spirit in disarray, which comes when surroundings are depressing and the mind is in despair.

The blues are the results of not being able to see the glory of the Easter sunrise, nor feel the warmth that comes from summer suns, while on sacred ancestral grounds.

When the colors of the evening sunset darken into an ill-favored tint and the skies produce no stars; there lay the blues.

When I can no longer sing high and lofty praises unto the Lord in my own tongue, because of my condition—my physical oppression and spiritual non-sensation; when hope has been replaced with glum, and dreams exchanged for nightmares, my soul sings the blues.

My soul becomes saddened when every common experience or signs of the Divine are destroyed—defaced by the hate and abuse of my enemies.

When the street signs are unfamiliar and the landscape is foreign,   . . . *I Sing The Blues*

III

By the rivers of Babylon, there we sat down,
yea we wept, when we remembered Zion,
We hanged our harps upon the willows in the midst
thereof.
For there they that carried us away captive required of us a song;
and they that wasted us required of us mirth, saying,
sing us one of the songs of Zion.
-Psalms 137

"How can we sing in a strange land?" The cries of Ancient blues singers, as they painfully hang their harps on weeping branches of the willow tree, their souls beclouded by their experience in captivity—their exile from Zion.

Yesterday; a fading keepsake: no jollity, old days of lark now gone, their sacred merriment, once renowned, only a passing remembrance of Zion.

Theirs were the blues—the song of the Diaspora; and with each refrain, one heard the song of pain, the drain and strain of slavery.

Even when the ancient dissolved into the modern, and the old grows faint and fades away, the blues—the song of the isolated—is ever present.

Each haunting chord invades the essence of each being—those whose life forces have been contaminated by their oppression.

"...How shall we sing the Lord's song in a strange land?"

IV

When Israel was in Egypt's land:
Oppressed so hard they could not stand,
No more shall they in bondage toil;
Let them come out with Egypt's spoil,
Go down Moses, 'Way down in Egypt land.
Tell ole Pharaoh, Let my people go!
-Go Down, Moses

Out of the ancient writ of Hebrew pilgrims comes a narrative, which flows out of a dim past. It whispers an old account of how the people of God recounts how their cries are overheard by the Eternal – *sub specie aeternitatis* – He being ever watchful, intercepted their cries. Their anguish, as a result of their plight in Egypt, stemmed from a shift in the affairs of state. An ominous current with its ill-wind brought forth a swelling tide of forced labor and economic repression.

Their oppression was not religious, but political. Labor without pay, bricks without straw—out of slavery came sonnets of sadness, hymns of grief. Theirs were the rondo of regret, especially when they recalled how it once had been in Egypt's land.

The songs of Sarah's children were not soured due to thoughts of transgression and sin; their chorus was coarse, because they now recalled their past station in Egypt. They were once an integrated part of the ancient mystic life and culture.

They were heart, mind and soul Kemites—Africans and their songs, once cheerful and gay, were the anthems of Egypt. But now, they lifted dirges of doom and despair, reveries to an estranged brother, "who knew not Joseph", and not their forgotten God.

So the message of brokenness was addressed to the state; it was not a prayer to the Divine. So at best, and to be sure—out of divine grace, the symphony of suffering, the blues of the Hebrews came to the Sublime on the wings of angels.

V

Sometimes I feel like a motherless chile,
Sometimes I feel like I'm almos' gone,
A long ways from home...
-Sometimes I Feel Like s Motherless Chile

For the sons and daughters of the Congo, Guinea, the banks of the Gold Coast and beyond—now shipwrecked on American soil, the blues is at best the harmonic anguish of a people—who wrestle with daily disappointment at life, and the oppressive reality which they face each day—while grappling with a temporary loss of faith.

For these castaways, what should have been at its worst, only a sonata—momentary movements describing their discomfort in captivity – became their oeuvre— lasting works of torment—wherein Divine language is mostly omitted. It is not a loss of faith in their God, nor His church; yet, their new hymn is an expression of an inability to articulate feelings through their faith, which was, and still is, being eclipsed daily as they enter into a new duality: "The un-enslaved" in a post slavery, secular, racist society.

Here the seeds of the Vanquished, in their pain and despair, searched for meaning beyond victimhood. Captured, enslaved and alienated, the no longer fully Africans found self-affirmation in a God – the son of a carpenter – a first century religious rebel—once a slave Himself; whom, on embrace, made them feel once again in touch with their humanity. This re-charted their soured notes, giving formation to spirituals and hymns. However, their social expression and dreams of achieving "all" that was promised after emancipation, and during their sharecropping epoch, was co-opted. A partition which was harsh and cruel appeared, offering no visible glimpse at the top or even a step above their existing condition.

Emancipation allowed the descendants of the newly let go, to go beyond physical slavery, but not beyond the color line and subjugation. Their pain, mixed with the sorrows of disappointment, turned what was to be a rose colored future into a blue one. The hypocrisy of the national church was enough to sour the souls of many *Colored Christians* against America's God, at least what God came to mean in the social expression and context of white Christianity.

Life beyond the plantation for the ex-enslaved brought them into contact with the new Canaanites; connecting them to a new culture which was beyond the moral tradition of the plantation church community. The hopes and promises of freedom depicted in the Spirituals were the impetus for seeking a new life, away from the sounds of chains, the sting of bullwhips, and the howling of hounds baying at night. But, the deep rooted and raw reality of racism was enough to change the tunes and lyrics of the newly freed, from the songs of Zion to a ditty of a disillusioned humanity—*The Blues.*

POETRY

The Constitutional Blues
del rio L.A. Blues
The Yule Tide Blues
Just Wondering
Getting It Too
No. 1
No. 2
No. 3
No. 4
I Saw Her Today
Premonition

The Constitutional Blues

Praised its enactment and lifted it to song,
With chorus: The 13th released us from harm.
In hindsight, for the seeds of Afrika it inked—
Increase passage to the institutional farm.
A new ghetto of concrete and iron bars—
Framed duly in constitutional law—
For the offspring of the Diaspora
The deal is still raw.
Can't fault the jurist,
Its what the framers said.
Offering three squares a day,
And some semblance of a bed;
Farbeit to say, its cruel and unusual—
Most whites are paroled—not released dead.
The 13th—a noble jester,
Or wickedness—shall the Bible advise?
Enslavement is still in this republic,
A quill: legalization—its mask, its disguise.

Three strikes or two,
Does it really matter?
Receiving one before recess,
HELL to the Chief, he vetoed the net and ladder.
"It shall not exist in these U.S., "
Students learn before the closing bell,
With cops out-numbering teachers in classes;
Today—learning is hell.
"Not in these U.S",
Except duly convicted by peers.
Prisons packed with young black boys,
Momma's eyes carry the biggest tears.
There's a new anthem now in the South,
And the North as well;
Sung by black babies—boys and girls,
　　　It's the blues,
—Its requiem drifts from their cells.

del rio L.A. Blues

Down at del rio L.A. smoking a blunt,
Trying my best to stay in the hunt;
There's no justifying my getting high,
Any excuse would just be a lie.

Things are rough and luck gone south,
Child support, back taxes, got no rent for the house;
It's a wonder I can put food in my mouth!

The gig I got, just won't do,
Just counting my old lady's needs, it takes two;
So sitting, I contemplate—drawing on this bamboo.

My mind is on fire with excrement from my past,
The blues from yesterday, still kicking my cash,
Not even the shrinks know how long it will last.

Twenty years in—no retirement in sight,
Economy in a tailspin; pillaged by pirates from the Right;
The Dow is on a gurney, can't even get it to spike,
Hell! Only a joint helps me sleep through the night.

Before grandma's funeral, hadn't been to church in years,
Heart broke to pieces—eyes full of tears,
The Lord met me in the cut—I was trying to chill;
Cousins still grinning, waiting to hear the will,

Faith—was a joint and a quart of gin,
If it wasn't for the Lord—I couldn't win;
Beyond the place, where I got nothin' to lose,

I'm no longer at the banks of del rio L.A.
—Singing the blues.

The Yule Tide Blues

Jingle Bells, Jingle Bells,
There's no children left to sing;
The County came at night—3 years ago,
    No knocks—not even a ring.
Jingle Bells, Jingle Bells,
The commotion could frighten a mouse;
An anonymous call—they said,
    Sent Case Workers to the house.
Lights spring on throughout the block,
As they took the children away;
Cops with them—"revolvers drawn,"
    You could hear the neighbors say.
There's no laughter, there's no fun,
As they ride to court each day;
The judge—bless her heart,
    Has signed, parental rights away.

No abuse: the report said later,
Young white teacher——"an innocent mistake;"
Not a burn, at first she thought,
    An allergy——a rare genetic trait;
The kids have problems in school today,
Three years in foster care;
Sexual abuse——the meds they take;
    Cause seizers and empty stares.
Jingle Bells, Jingle Bells,
Parenting While Black——no Christmas cheers;
Yule tide- no longer sung,
    Only The Blues——mixed with tears.

Just Wondering

I wonder,
      If Jamaicans get the blues?
I can imagine that they too, have paid their dues,
But irie man! They seem to relax,
I wonder if their grandfathers paid poll tax?
They don't seem to move to the same tune,
      Singing Rasta;
Blowing on that ganja up to noon;
They party like us and we all smoke that stuff,
I was just wondering,

                  …Just thinking off the cuff.
Sometimes I wonder if they hear our dark sound?
      We know—
They get risked and patted down,
Like us they're stopped while cruising down the block—
The difference—

               …Their Healey suffered vapor lock.
But the blues they don't seem to sing,
      As they be-bop away—
Down M.L. King;
Yet they work hard and drink their booze,
I still wonder—

                …If they too, get the blues?
I just wonder if Jamaicans get the blues—like I?
      Wearing colors that scream,
Drinking rum punch, eating mincemeat pie;
Black tones to high yellow skin—we all share that tattoo.
I understand their pride,

            …But do they get the blues too?

It's hard to imagine Jamaicans,
    Feel pain like we who eat greens,
Is it that they have more in common, with—
Those English Queens?
Maybe having your own Island—knowing Cricket rules,
Muffles ones reality,
                      ...No cause to sing the blues.

Should Jamaicans be held in contempt?
    If the blues they wish not to sing,
Nor even attempt;
Flossin, rapping— perpetrating all day,
Has not rescued us,
                    ...Nor chased our blues away.

If they don't sing the blues,
It's alright with me,
    Especially when I see,
How pretty—Jamaicans girls can be.

Getting It Too

No. 1

For Donna,
The blues was being dropped from list — A to below Z,
Her divorce from John,
Canceled her RSVP.
It seems that Ed's Oscar party,
She had attended for years,
Was now off limits—
Excuse—to avoid emotional tears.
In Hollywood,
Where films end in bliss,
Donna and others now sings the blues, their names—
...Keeps appearing on *"The Don't Come"* list.

No. 2

The blues for Uncle Charlie,
Was an acquired taste,
With old canned sardines and,
Soft saltines he made into paste.
Cotton picking days,
Not in the south but Bakersfield,
He planned on getting paid—didn't know—
Bad wine was in the deal.
With harmonica in hand,
Central Ave, replaced the rows and the dust,
But Charlie's acquisition of the blues remained,
...So did his taste for rotgut.

No. 3

For Elian's uncle
Whose 60 seconds of fame, has disappeared,
Comes words denying asylum—
His blues—now mixed with tears.
His clan led the exiles
Giving new lyrics to an old freedom song,
But, 8 millions dollars later—
Elian is now back home.
On Thanksgiving Day
He arrived riding on a tube,
Floating with little Elian,
…The tide also brought the blues.

No. 4

The Teddy of ol'
Said that the blues was a thing of the past,
Perhaps for him, but for most brothers—
The melody still lingers and last.
Driving while black,
And gunned down in the dark,
Even Ray Charles could see—
The blues has found no new mark.
'Everyday I have the blues,'
Is a tune most brothers know well;
It may be kinder, gentler for some—
But for us this republic,
...Is still hell!

I Saw Her Today

I saw the blues today.
She stopped,
Stared,
And smiled,
But thank God,
She decided not to stay.

Premonition

I have come to this place before,
Something foreboding, I perceive—
Lurking behind the door.
I've smelled its scent in the air,
Shattered dreams, broken hearts—
Lives thrown in despair.
I've sensed its presence — I've felt its stare,
Cunning, calculating; a chill from the past;
T'was the blues, an old adversary,
...I'd know him anywhere.

When The Heart Bleeds Blue: *The Search For Love*

PROSE

When The Heart Bleeds Blue

I

"I sit in my chair
I'm filled with despair
There's no one could be so sad
With gloom ev'rywhere
I sit and I stare
I know that I'll soon go mad"
-"Solitude" ...Ellington, Delange, Miles

The African American struggle to find his or her song apart from the blues, is not only one of discovering human clarity in the American life, but being social beings, it is also the hunt or outward search for soul mates to be a companion voice—one, when harmonized—would bring a new part to life, to existence; thus creating a new song, one of brightness and love.

Both the pre-voyage and post-journey experience of the Atlantic trade of captured Africans created more than a heritage of enslavement, it raped and ravaged its most sacred commodity. It breached the respect and sacredness of the African husband and wife and that which they once held supreme towards one another.

The system said in so many ways to the African male now in chains, "never again hope to be a vital part and play a respectful or key role in the life and affairs of the African woman who shares the same fate." And as if with amusement, it jested that beyond the already limited involvement, it further decreed that the choices of human love, companionship and intimacy for the Nubian male and female, was now cruelly out of their hands.

II

By night on my bed I sought him whom my soul loveth:
I sought him, but I found him not.
I will rise now, and go about the city
in the streets, and in the broad ways
I will seek him whom my soul loveth:
I sought him, but I found him not.
- The Song of Solomon 3:1,2

We have found that our lonely search has pushed us along rocky and sometimes barren trails, through pained moments of conflict, trials, and disappointments. Being alone conjures yesteryears ghosts of false judgments and abuses, all the while in search of that voice, a true voice that matches our own.

    "...Dear Lord above; send back my love."

III

This bitter earth, what fruit it bears
What good is love; that no one shares?
And if my life is like the dust,
that hides the glow...
What good am I?
Heaven only knows.
-"This Bitter Earth"...Clyde Otis

Like Adam, even terrestrial paradises are merely deserts for the heart, a hellish sod, that can only be transformed by like kind, some lover whose kisses are sincere enough to banish the pain of today's trials and abuse; gentle enough to soften the scabs of my unjustified punishment.

I have had the blues, howbeit; there is no blues like the malformed tune, not quite a song that is yanked out of an oppressed heart. Its crippled notes and disfigured lyrics are squeezed out, twisted, and mangled, leaving in its wake—a faint semblance of what once was.

...Yes, I sing the Blues.

POETRY

The Long Search
The Blues Is...
Fear
Wearing It Well
The Wind Sings Love
Deez
The Cure For My Blues

The Long Search

"I guess you'll be looking for a place!"
I had not realized, she so closely observed,
The dithering rhythm of my pace—
Since 1619 I've been in haste!
To find my way back to where
My identity is based.
Long ago I lengthened my strive,
Searching for that place
Where I could come alive.

"How long will it take?"
Long enough I thought,
To finish this race;
The prize—ancestral images - I need to trace!
Roots that speak the truth— we
Were a people steeped in supernatural grace.

"Will you be looking for another spot?"
Yes! Far from those memories
Where the souls of my fathers were laid to rot.
Somewhere I can call home,
Where my spirit can be at peace,
And my soul no longer needs to roam.
There's a tame terrain—I saw in a dream,
Where those of my likeness,
Were not trained to be mean.

"Are you looking for a place?"
Came something dissimilar in her voice,
A tone of authority,
That said I had no other choice.
Now I need a place to stay,
Here we go again, I just can't win!
Power she had—from plantation days—
Ode to the system—it's intact to the end.

The Blues Is...

The blues is the color of the hole,
That occupies the emptiness of my soul.
It is the voice that replaced my cheers;
A cacophony—mingled with tears.
It is the specter that walks the floors with me at night,
The uninvited—whose offering is just another vice.
The blues crawls to me, so I won't be—alone;
It's the smeared colors of the lips—
...Now, that you're gone.

Fears

There is this, that runs the breath of me,
It probes the depths—even my dreams,
It dares question the notions of what
You and I could be.

It lays my fears open wide,
Descending each level of my soul,
My insecurities are no longer concealed—
All the things I've attempted to hide.

Rejection—fear and pain it brings,
Trapped with thoughts that my best,
Is far less than the rest—see now the
Bruises—left from this scorpion's sting.

Still—there remains this theme—
Embracing, imparting, inspiring me,
With truth—a song that angels only hope
To sing: 'your love is more than a dream.'

Wearing It Well

She said—I wore the blues well,
I thought she spoke of shades and colors,
But I was too immature to tell.
She said—I wore the blues well,
That it became me and suited my complexion.
I imagined she referred to looks,
But vanity can send understanding,
In the wrong direction—
She said—I wore the blues well,
And her attractiveness, age and accent—
Kinda sorta set the mood.
I took it as a gesture and pursued,
It was only then, I realized, that the blues
        was the color of—
...A real live ATTITUDE!

The Wind Sings Love

The wind sung to me today,
With songs of love and hope—sincere;
Lyrics so refreshing, the leaves gently moved,
So the wind could bring its song near.
The wind sung to me today,
Melodies without ill colors, nor hints of blue—
A song, full of passion with perfect reframe,
Gently—softly whispering that love can be true.
The wind brought music today,
Full of laughter and joy;
The notes charted, awakened my soul,
Your love is the reason—
—That I'm whole.

Deez

Deez are the dreams that appear in
The night,
Ushering my blues far from
My sight.
Deez nights' alone thinking
Of you,
Conjure thoughts of what it would please me
To do—
Deez eyes of mine miss
Your grace,
And the countenance of your
Celestial face.
Deez lips remembers the sweetness
Of yours,
With delight tremble they—wishing
For more—
And Deez arms of mine long to hold,
And envelope you once again,
Only you, prompted by your heart
And soul, can tell me—
      WHEN!

The Cure For My Blues

Consider this to be true
It's more than a notion—I miss you.
For it's more than a whisper,
My soul aches & echoes like thunder;
Is it real that absence
     Does cause the heart to grow fonder?
Consider this thought too
Not a day passes—I don't long to be with you;
Grave is your image,
That visits & haunts from time to time,
For the love we shared
     Stays on my mind.
Consider this, for it is true
Love again—I tried to paint,
With artistry of brilliant hues,
Yet when framed & hung—on viewing,
     The portrait is always of you.
And when all is considered,
This should not be new news,
Your face, your smile, your love,
Has always been the cure—
     —For my blues.